D0780095

ABRAHAM & MARY TODD LINCOLN

Margaret Bassett

a volume in
Profiles and Portraits of
American Presidents and Their Wives
Series

The Bond Wheelwright Company *Publishers* · Porter's Landing, Freeport, Maine

CONTENTS

LIST OF ILLUSTRATIONS

Photo by Winfred "Doc" Helm and Arthur "Boots" Holland

In all his life Abraham Lincoln owned but one home. Originally a small one-and-a-half story cottage, by 1857 it had been remodeled to a full two-story house. It stands on the northeast corner of Eighth and Jackson streets in Springfield, Illinois, looking today nearly as it did when Lincoln left for the White House in Washington, D.C., on February 11, 1861. Note the restored wooden sidewalk to the right of the house and the outbuildings behind it. There Lincoln kept his horse, buggy, cow, and a good supply of fuel for his horses. Today Lincoln's home is a State shrine and is open to the public. In keeping with Lincoln's practice, the building is painted light brown.

THE PRESIDENCY

The Presidency of the United States, as a repository of both power and prestige, is unique in the world. Its occupant is chief of state, head of government, and commander of the armed forces. Beyond these formal roles, well-rooted in the Constitution, are powerful ones, which were unplanned for, and yet have been played by the Chief Executives since the beginning of our national history. The Presidents have frequently been our moral leaders, the fountainheads of patriotism, the principal source of information and news, and our pace-setters in everything from personal courage to cultural tastes. Above all, they have provided the dramatic emphases of our story as a people.

The office of President is a continuous one in the legal sense, but the special qualities its incumbents have brought in turn to it, invest it with its vibrancy and, indeed, its majesty. Each new President exhibits a style of behavior, a quality of insight and determination, and a measure of personal magnetism that marks his place in history—ours and the world's. When a man yields up the keys of this office to his successor, there is heard no equivalent of the ancient cry, "The King is dead, Long live the King!" Presidents are not interchangeable or standardized parts of our political system, and we are instinctively sure that we would not have them so.

The Presidents who parade before us, in turn, cannot escape being subject to constant public scrutiny and criticism, and then, historical evaluation. How we judge the individual Chief Executives is, of course, a matter of our own politics, our sense of the past, and the fact that we are Americans. Some appear larger than life—and some smaller. It seems unavoidable that we make our President into what we want him to be. We ascribe to him the qualities we prize most in

1

ourselves. The effect has been that the President often seems to reflect the America of his time with an uncanny precision, which, considering the vagaries of the political obstacle course he runs to reach the White House, is truly remarkable. It makes of the presidency a delicate, indispensable instrument of republican government that far surpasses anything in the most optimistic dreams of the Founding Fathers.

Every schoolchild, if he learns nothing else of American history, learns the names of all the Presidents and fixes in his mind the faces of the most important of them. One thing, therefore, he is made aware of early: our nation is still so young that unlike the Kings of France or the Sultans of Turkey, the Presidents of the United States each occupy a niche and are identified with a record that the well-informed citizen must consult. One day, as our history lengthens, it will no longer be possible to know in intimate detail the lives of the Presidents any more than the ordinary well-informed person today can know, let us say, the lives of the Saints. Until then, however, the careers of our Chief Executives, like their faces, will be recognized individually.

The history of the presidency, nevertheless, is no mere kaleidoscope of faces changing in endless procession. Even now the men who have served as our Chief Executives and whose deeds are celebrated here are beginning to fall into definable groups.

Four of the first five Presidents—Washington, Jefferson, Madison, and Monroe—were Virginia "aristocrats." They had had a vigorous part in creating the new government and they were uncompromisingly committed to making it a success—in Washington's memorable words, to establishing "a standard to which the wise and honest can repair." The society out of which they sprang did not fully embrace "the people." Its spokesmen generally regarded the ownership of property as a basic requirement for voting and for holding office, and they never used the word "democracy" in a benign sense, preferring to think of it as a synonym for mob rule.

If these viewpoints seem repellent or even in-comprehensible today, it must be remembered that joined with them was a deeply felt obligation to participate in

2

unselfish public service as a way of life. This kind of dynamic for power motivated also John and John Quincy Adams of Massachusetts, who added to the Virginia ideal a pessimism about human nature, drawn from their New England heritage, that sometimes made both father and son seem crabbed and uncharitable. Most important, the first six Presidents, like Old Testament patriarchs, served their conception of what constituted the public good without currying popularity or enslaving themselves to that remarkable master, whose power had not yet been discovered, "the will of the majority."

The inauguration of Andrew Jackson in 1829 began a new phase in the history of the Executive Office. Jackson was the beneficiary of the discovery of "the people," who in larger numbers than ever before were going to the polls to express electoral choices. Never thereafter would public policies—including especially those emanating from the White House—be presented as being what the nation ought to have, but instead, as what the people want.

Yet in the thirty years that followed Jackson's advent it was not always easy for a President to pander to or satisfy this emerging "democratic spirit." The tendency was for citizens to look to Congress rather than to the Chief Executive for the satisfaction they required. Although a number of the first fifteen Presidents were held in high esteem everywhere in the expanding country (and Washington and Jackson were revered figures), there was a widespread fear of government, expressed as a fear of a strong executive branch. The American recollection of George III faded slowly.

The Civil War and the herculean part that Abraham Lincoln played in it brought a change. A President, it seemed, could combine humanity with power, wage a modern war relentlessly but magnanimously, and preserve the constitutional structure under mortal attack. Lincoln's presidency became a new and inspiring model for occupants of the office. His immediate successors, however, were both products and victims of the rapid industrialization of America and the postwar letdown in the morality of public officeholders.

The opening of the Twentieth Century coincided almost

3

exactly with the accession of Theodore Roosevelt to the presidency. T. R. entered the national scene on the wings of America's seemingly easy victory over Spain in 1898. He brought youthfulness, unquenchable energy, and a keen sense of the direction in which "public opinion"—a phenomenon produced in part by the emergence of mass journalism—was leading the nation. He created the pattern that still is dominant in our conception of how a Chief Executive ought to comport himself, modified, to be sure, by the favorites who came after him—Wilson, Franklin Roosevelt, Eisenhower, Truman, and Kennedy.

From T. R.'s time to the present, the Presidents have been moving closer and closer to the people they serve. Although Lincoln was the first who was widely photographed, it was not until the newspaper halftone became a commonplace after 1900 that the President's face could regularly be seen in every home and with a variety of expressions. Then came the motion picture, which could show the President in action, the radio, which could bring his voice to every hearthside, and the television set, which could make him a veritable visitor in every living room. Moreover, the transcendent events that have occurred on the scene beyond our water's edge have made the Presidents of the United States world figures, whose comings and goings are of moment everywhere. Their policies, their family life, even their physical condition, have a reach into every corner of the earth. And when they leave the immedicate scene they are remembered in foreign lands, not only through the statues and street names that daily recall their labors, but in programs and utterances like the Monroe Doctrine in the Nineteenth Century and the Truman Doctrine in our own, the Fourteen Points of Woodrow Wilson, the Four Freedoms of Franklin Roosevelt, Dwight Eisenhower's Atoms for Peace, and many others. Jefferson's prediction—"The election of a President of America, some years hence, will be much more interesting to certain nations of Europe, than ever the election of a King of Poland was"—has been gloriously fulfilled.

HENRY F. GRAFF

4

ABRAHAM LINCOLN, Sixteenth President

(The Republican party)in 1860 had wider support, more verve, a better list of candidates for the presidential nomination, and a better chance of defeating the Democrats than on its trial run four years earlier. It also had a great wooden building, called "The Wigwam" for its nominating convention in Chicago, with room for upwards of 10,000 of the general public to watch the proceedings. The leading candidate, the one with the largest personal following in the party and the man who certainly deserved his party's highest honor, was William H. Seward of New York. When the convention got down to the business of balloting, it was plain that Seward lacked the votes to win. In the opinion of the general public that packed the balcony, the man to nominate was the lawyer from Springfield, the man who out-talked Douglas in '58, "Honest Old Abe." On the third ballot the convention made the people in the balcony uproariously happy by nominating Lincoln. A cannon on the roof of the Wigwam boomed and the crowds outside joined the cheering.

Seward, the accomplished politician and defeated favorite, called him contemptuously the "prairie statesman" and Lincoln's campaign managers welcomed any picturesque phrase that emphasized the commonness, the rusticity of the man. They steered the campaign as close to the Jacksonian and log-cabin tradition as they possibly could, while Lincoln himself stayed at home receiving visitors but making no speeches. His campaign speeches had been made long since, beginning in 1854 when he undertook to campaign for one Richard Yates running for Congress in Illinois and including the debates with the little Democrat Stephen Douglas in 1858. In the Douglas debates he was running for Douglas's seat in the United States Senate and he had lost the race. But it was the Lincoln speeches that still echoed across the nation and it

5

was Lincoln who had forced Douglas to give up his claim to leadership in the Democratic party.

(The six years of his great speeches)summed up with classic simplicity Lincoln's arguments against slavery. They indicted the South for retrogressing in its handling of the

The earliest known portrait of Lincoln, taken in 1847, by Nicholas Shepherd, itinerant daguerreotypist, in Springfield. Lincoln was then Congressman-elect from Illinois.

6

slaves; they posed the issue politically as one capable of reasonable solution; and they rejected the emotionalism of the radical abolitionists. With a distilled clarity, and without the rolling periods of rich language generally loved by orators, they made excellent reading, as they still do. For instance, in a speech at Peoria in 1854: "Near eighty years ago we began by declaring that all men are created equal; but now, from that beginning, we have run down to the other declaration, that for some men to enslave others is a 'sacred right of self-government.' These principles cannot stand together. They are as opposite as God and Mammon." And in accepting the Republican nomination for the Senate in 1858: " 'A house divided against itself cannot stand.' I believe this government cannot endure permanently half slave and half free. I do not expect the Union to be dissolved—I do not expect the house to fall—but I do expect it will cease to be divided. It will become all one thing or all the other. Either the opponents of slavery will arrest the further spread of it, and place it where the public mind shall rest in the belief that it is in course of ultimate extinction; or its advocates will push it forward till it shall become alike lawful in all the States, old as well as new, North as well as South."

The emergence of genius is as mysterious when it appears in politics as it is in other forms of art. Abraham Lincoln was born about as humbly as possible. Every shred of evidence relating to his family and early life has been tenderly gathered together and interpreted. Much of it is good reading and good, honest folklore. The simple facts are that he was born on a farm near present-day Hodgenville, of a poor frontier family that never took hold of the land and settled down. When he was seven they moved on to Indiana and began clearing a quarter section deep in the forest near a crossroads that became known as Gentryville. Here his mother died and Abe acquired a stepmother, a kind woman who sympathized with the boy's restless desire for knowledge. The opportunities for education were almost nil—Lincoln later estimated that he had had not more than twelve months of schooling in all his life—but occasionally the boy got hold of a book, and no matter what it was, he read it avidly. At the same time he

7

grew remarkably tall (six feet, four inches) and strong. He was a great hand with an axe or a plow, but he was also very gentle, a great talker, and somewhat lazy.

When Lincoln was twenty-one he helped his family move to Illinois and build a cabin on the Sangamon River, then set out to make his own living. He came to rest for a few years at New Salem, a nondescript little settlement near Springfield, which a few years later was abandoned. Here he clerked in a store and tried to operate a store of his own, a financial disaster that kept him in debt for seventeen years. He met the

Part of a page of math from Lincoln's exercise book. At the lower left, he has written: "Abraham Lincoln
his hand and pen
he will be good but
god knows When."

From Lincoln's autobiographical sketch, written in the third person (ca. June 1860), for John Locke Scripps of the Chicago Press & Tribune, who used it as the basis for a campaign biography:
. . . A. now thinks that the aggregate of all his schooling did not amount to one year. He was never in a college or academy as a student; and never inside of a college or academy building till since he had a law license. What he has in the way of education, he has picked up. After he was twenty-three, and had separated from his father, he studied English grammar, imperfectly of course, but so as to speak and write as well as he now does. He studied and nearly mastered the six books of Euclid, since he was a member of Congress. He regrets his want of education and does what he can to supply the want . . .

young toughs of Clary's Grove and wrestled their leader Jack Armstrong. He fell in love with Anne Rutledge and went through a period of black melancholy when she died. He was debating whether he should become a blacksmith or aspire to the law, for which he feared he had too little education, when he ran successfully for the Illinois legislature, where he was to serve for the next eight years.

The legislature opened up a new life. He was soon borrowing law books, licensed to practice and part of a law firm. In 1837 he moved to Springfield, the same year it became capital of the state, an event that he had helped to bring about in the legislature. Here for the first time he enjoyed the society, and approval, of educated people.

From Lincoln's autobiographical sketch:

. . . The election of 1834 came, and he was then elected to the legislature by the highest vote cast for any candidate. Major John T. Stuart, then in full practice of the law, was also elected. During the canvass, in a private conversation he encouraged A. to study law. After the election he borrowed books of Stuart, took them home with him, and went at it in good earnest. He studied with nobody. He still mixed in the surveying to pay board and clothing bills. When the legislature met, the law books were dropped, but were taken up again at the end of the session. He was re-elected in 1836, 1838, and 1840. In the autumn of 1836 he obtained a law license, and on April 15, 1837, removed to Springfield, and commenced the practice, his old friend, Stuart taking him into partnership. March 3rd, 1837, by a protest entered upon the Ills. House Journal of that date, at pages 817, 818, A. with Dan Stone, another representative of Sangamon, briefly defined his position on the slavery question; and so far as it goes, it was then the same that is is now. The protest is as follows—

March 3, 1837

Resolutions upon the subject of domestic slavery having passed both branches of the General Assembly at its present session, the undersigned hereby protest against the passage of the same.

They believe that the institution of slavery is founded on both injustice and bad policy; but that the promulgation of abolition doctrines tends rather to increase than to abate its evils.

They believe that the Congress of the United States has no power, under the constitution, to interfere with the institution of slavery in the different states.

They believe that the Congress of the United States has the power, under the constitution, to abolish slavery in the District of Columbia; but that that power ought not to be exercized unless at the request of the people of said District.

The difference between these opinions and those contained in the said resolutions, is their reason for entering this protest.

Physically he was ungainly—at first impression downright ugly—with overlong arms, large hands and feet. His hair was black and untidy and his swarthy face rested usually in an expression of melancholy. But he won people with his immense kindness and a patent honesty that he was inclined to mix with humor. As a lawyer, he might not be particularly learned, but he had a pointed way of putting his case and an analytical mind that disrobed an argument of its sophistry with unerring skill. He was popular among men as a good talker and a great storyteller. With women he was inclined to go into emotional somersaults, but finally, after five years in Springfield and an interrupted engagement, he capitulated to Mary Todd, a very eligible young girl who had set her heart on him.

For several years after marriage, Lincoln devoted himself to a deeper study and practice of law, interrupted only by a single term in the United States House of Representatives, as a Whig. The slavery issue, which had been quiescent after the Clay compromises of 1850, suddenly burst into flame with the passage of Douglas's Kansas-Nebraska Act. This act, an unwarranted victory for the pro-slavery South, repealed the Missouri Compromise of 1820 that had declared the northwest territories free, and theoretically at least, made them available for settlers with slaves.

The effect on Lincoln was to arouse him from the complacency of his prosperous life, stirring up his political antagonism to Douglas and his sense of outrage at the Southern attack on the principle of human fairness, a cornerstone of his own temperament. In the fall of 1854 he

---

Abraham Lincoln, in an editorial offered to the editors of the Illinois Journal *on the issue of the Kansas-Nebraska law:*
The state of the case in a few words, is this: The Missouri Compromise excluded slavery from the Kansas-Nebraska territory. The repeal opened the territories to slavery. If there is any meaning to the declaration in the 14th section, that it does not mean to legislate slavery into the territories, it is this: that it does not require slaves to be sent there. The Kansas and Nebraska territories are now as open to slavery as Mississippi or Arkansas were when they were territories.

To illustrate the case: Abraham Lincoln has a fine meadow, containing beautiful springs of water, and well fenced, which John

looked ahead, sometimes with confidence, to an office he was peculiarly fitted to occupy.

Lincoln's inaugural address was extraordinarily mild. He tried to reassure the South on its rights and persuade it that it was easier to get on with the North inside the Union than outside. While he bent every effort to constrict the geography of secession and keep in the Union the states that had not seceded, he made not the slightest motion toward military preparation. Never a man to be hurried, he waited for Virginia to make up her mind, while he was plagued to decide what to do about Fort Sumter, isolated, with its Federal garrison, in Charleston Harbor in South Carolina, the first state to secede. By the end of March, Lincoln decided, though most of the cabinet disagreed, that Sumter had to be held as a matter of principle, and he ordered a relief expedition to it.

From Abraham Lincoln's first inaugural address, March 4, 1861:
. . . Physically speaking we cannot separate. We cannot remove our respective sections from each other, nor build an impassable wall between them. A husband and wife may be divorced, and go out of the presence, and beyond the reach of each other; but the different parts of our country cannot do this. They cannot but remain face to face; and intercourse, either amicable or hostile, must continue between them. Is it possible then to make that intercourse more advantageous, or more satisfactory, *after* separation than *before?* . . .

My countrymen, one and all, think calmly and *well*, upon this whole subject. Nothing valuable can be lost by taking time. If there be an object to *hurry* any of you, in hot haste, to a step which you would never take *deliberately*, that object will be frustrated by taking time; but no good object can be frustrated by it. Such of you as are now dissatisfied, still have the old Constitution unimpaired, and, on the sensitive point, the laws of your own framing under it; while the new administration will have no immediate power, if it would, to change either. If it were admitted that you who are dissatisfied, hold the right side in the dispute, there still is no single good reason for precipitate action. Intelligence, patriotism, Christianity, and a firm reliance on Him, who has never yet forsaken this favored land, are still competent to adjust, in the best way, all our present difficulty.

In *your* hands, my dissatisfied fellow-countrymen, and not in *mine*, is the momentous issue of civil war. The government will not assail *you*. You can have no conflict, without being yourselves the aggressors. *You* have no oath registered in Heaven to destroy the government, while *I* shall have the most solemn one to "preserve, protect and defend" it.

I am loath to close. We are not enemies, but friends. We must not be enemies. Though passion may have strained, it must not break our bonds of affection. The mystic chords of memory, stretching from every battlefield, and patriot grave, to every living heart and hearthstone, all over this broad land, will yet swell the chorus of the Union, when again touched, as surely they will be, by the better angels of our nature.

13

The Confederate government now hesitated between war and peace, and Major Anderson in the fort offered to surrender in three days if he were not provisioned or ordered to hold on by Washington. Anderson was the precipitant to Jefferson Davis's worries. The Confederate president was trying to decide whether secession would succeed better with a clash of arms. In the end he took the war gamble, ordering General Beauregard, Confederate commander at Charleston, to fire on the fort if there was an attempt to reinforce it. Some of Beauregard's officers took matters in their own hands and began the bombardment on April twelfth.

There was an enthusiasm in the North for the war. Men enlisted readily in the first draft call, and the militia regiments

Highlights of Lincoln's Administration

The caption of this John Tenniel cartoon, commenting on Lincoln's decision to avoid a clash with the British in the *Trent* affair, read:

"UP A TREE"
Colonel Bull and the Yankee 'Coon.
'Coon: "Air you in arnest, Colonel?"
Colonel Bull: "I am."
'Coon: "Don't fire—I'll come down."

The Civil War. The first shot was fired at Fort Sumter in Charleston Harbor, April 12, 1861, the fort surrendering after 34 hours. The states that made up the Confederate States of America were South Carolina, Georgia, Alabama, Mississippi, Louisiana, Florida, Texas, Arkansas, Virginia, North Carolina, Tennessee. The border states Missouri, Kentucky, Maryland, and the western counties of Virginia (West Virginia) stayed in the Union. Confederate General Robert E. Lee surrendered at Appomattox Court House, Virginia, April 9, 1865, and the rest of the Confederate armies surrendered in the succeeding weeks, the last May twenty-sixth. Casualties: 360,000 Union soldiers died; 258,000 Confederate soldiers died; 500,000 wounded on both sides.

The *Trent* Affair. Confederate agents Mason and Slidell, on their way to London and Paris on the British mailship *Trent*, were taken off and brought back to the United States by the American naval ship *San Jacinto*. Great Britain claimed violation of a neutral ship. Lincoln maintained the right to search British vessels but released Mason and Slidell and the tension between the two countries eased.

turned out in their fine uniforms, marching gaily off to war with the cry "On to Richmond!" confident that they would roll right over the "secesh" army and settle matters in a hurry. It was not to be. Lincoln lacked good military advice and good general officers. After the brave new army was thrown back disgracefully at the Battle of Bull Run on July twenty-first in the first summer, the word was "more training." Lincoln selected a young West Pointer named George McClellan to train the army. This he did, magnificently, but he never led it

Entered according to act of Congress, in the year 1862, by ALEX. GARDNER, in the Clerk's Office of the District Court of the District of Columbia.

GARDNER, Photographer.   M. B. BRADY, Publisher.

THE PRESIDENT AND GENERAL McCLELLAN

On the Battle-field of Antietam.

October 4, 1862.

to victory. In all, the army that started out for Richmond was in the hands of five successive commanders and was a very different army before it marched into Richm   ' nearly four years later. It was not until March of 1864   General Ulysses S. Grant came from his successful western c   rns to supply the kind of over-all military command that   win the war.

The caption for this copper-plate engraving by Adelbert J. Volck, Confederate caricaturist, read: The President and his players "come to play a pleasant comedy, a kind of history." Chase, Secretary of the Treasury, is at the window. Cameron, Secretary of War, is the puppet whose wire runs through the highest hole. Welles, Secretary of the Navy, rows the boat, and back of him is General Butler. The three other generals, in the foreground, are Fremont, Scott, and McClellan.

A Mathew Brady portrait of General Grant at Cold Harbor, Virginia in 1864

In the long search for a winning general, Lincoln showed restraint and patience. The same qualities made him a superb civil administrator. He had in his cabinet several able but difficult men. These he handled with the authority of a dictator and the understanding of a house mother, and was rewarded by their becoming hard-working department heads. He was concerned at all times that the war objective should be understood: to restore the Union. He did intend that slavery should be abolished, with compensation if possible, but the restless and mischievous abolitionists who accused him of going too slowly on slavery were severely and plainly reprimanded. However, he came to believe that the moral position of the war effort at home and abroad required a move toward emancipation. Therefore, in September 1862, after the Union army turned back the Confederate invasion of Maryland at Antietam, Lincoln issued the preliminary emancipation proclamation.

Highlights of Lincoln's Administration

Great Britain's permitting the secret building of ships for the Confederate navy in British shipyards. Lincoln protested through the American minister Charles Francis Adams. After laborious representations by Adams the practice was stopped, but the *Florida* and *Alabama*, Confederate raiders built in England, destroyed $15,000,000 worth of Union ships and cargo.

Financing the War: In 1861, a 3 per cent income tax was declared on incomes over $800, and a direct tax and quarter-billion-dollar loan authorized.

The Legal Tender Act of February 25, 1862, making "Greenbacks" or Treasury notes legal tender for all dues except imports and interest on the public debt, and a half-billion dollar loan. More greenbacks were authorized by Congress later. Also further loans.

The National Banking Act, of February 25, 1863, amended 1864: a national banking system by which member banks invested a third of their capital in government bonds and were allowed to issue notes up to 90 per cent of the value of those bonds. A minimum of capital stock and of cash reserves was set and stockholders were held responsible for a proportion of bank's debts. This system drove most of the old state banks out of business.

The preliminary emancipation proclamation, September 23, 1862, that all slaves in states in rebellion would be free on January 1, 1863. On January first a final proclamation, by military authority, declared free slaves in all the South except Tennessee and the parts of Louisiana and Virginia held by Union armies. Because the proclamation was probably not legal under civil law, the Thirteenth Amendment to the Constitution was introduced in Congress, March 28, 1864. It had passed both houses by January 31, 1865. It was declared ratified on December 18, 1865.

ONE GOOD TURN DESERVES ANOTHER.

The above cartoon by John Tenniel appeared in *Punch,* the famous British satirical weekly, before Lincoln issued his preliminary emancipation proclamation.

The final Emancipation Proclamation read in part:

. . . by virtue of the power and for the purpose aforesaid, I do order and declare that all persons held as slaves within said designated States, and parts of States, are, and henceforward shall be free; and that the executive government of the United States, including the military and naval authorities thereof, will recognize and maintain the freedom of said persons.

And I hereby enjoin upon the people so declared to be free to abstain from all violence, unless in necessary self-defence; and I recommend to them that, in all cases when allowed, they labor faithfully for reasonable wages.

And I further declare and make known, that such persons of suitable condition, will be received into the armed service of the United States to garrison forts, positions, stations, and other places, and to man vessels of all sorts in said service.

And upon this act, sincerely believed to be an act of justice, warranted by the Constitution, upon military necessity, I invoke the considerate judgment of mankind, and the gracious favor of Almighty God . . .

19

Above: An artist's conception of the New York Provost Guard attacking draft rioters on 2nd Avenue.

Right:The subject of the draft was a topic for cartoons even before the conscription law was enacted. The original caption below this *Harper's Weekly* (11/2/1862) cartoon read: "All other Methods of evading the Draft having failed, the above Disgraceful Scheme is to be attempted on the 10th."

Courtesy Library of Congress

Highlights of Lincoln's Administration

The conscription law of March 3, 1863, drafting all male citizens between ages of twenty and forty-five. Badly written, it permitted those with money to buy off from a particular summons or to provide a substitute to fill their places in the roll. It was hardest on the poor. On July thirteenth, draft riots began in New York and lasted for four days, during which a thousand were killed or injured and a number of buildings were looted and burned.

Dedication of the Military Cemetery at Gettysburg, November 19, 1863, for which Lincoln delivered the Gettysburg Address.

This is how Abraham Lincoln looked to his constituents during the bloody Civil War. The photographer for this portrait was Alexander Gardner of Washington, D.C. It was made on November 8, 1863, only a few days before Lincoln made his noble address at Gettysburg. Usually this photograph is shown only as a head and shoulders of Lincoln, but Mr. Ostendorf discovered that it had more to it and it is shown here as Gardner took it.

The 1864 presidential campaign came in the last gloomy summer of the war. More than a few people, including pontifical Horace Greeley of the New York *Tribune,* doubted that Lincoln could be elected unless the Confederate armies were beaten speedily. For once Lincoln agreed with him. The North was mortally dispirited and even here and there disaffected. But Sherman's capture of Atlanta on September third was a tonic and by election day there was a general confidence that the war was going to be won. Lincoln, renominated by the Republicans, or the "National Union party," was handsomely re-elected and with him as Vice-President, Andrew Johnson of Tennessee. His second inaugural address included the unforgettable paragraph beginning: "With malice toward none; with charity for all; with firmness in the right, as God gives us to see the right, let us strive on to finish the work we are in; to bind up the nation's wounds. . . ."

Frank Bellew's caricature appeared in Harper's Weekly after President Lincoln's re-election, with the apt title: "Long Abe a Little Longer."

Lincoln's second inaugural address:
March 4, 1865
Fellow-Countrymen:
At this second appearing to take the oath of the presidential office, there is less occasion for an extended address than there was at the first. Then a statement, somewhat in detail, of a course to be pursued, seemed fitting and proper. Now, at the expiration of four years, during which public declarations have been constantly called forth on every point and phase of the great contest which still absorbs the attention, and engrosses the energies of the nation, little that is new could be presented. The progress of our arms, upon which all else chiefly depends, is as well known to the public as to myself; and it is I trust, reasonably satisfactory and encouraging to all. With high hope for the future, no prediction in regard to it is ventured.
On the occasion corresponding to this four years ago, all thoughts were anxiously directed to an impending civil war. All dreaded it—all sought to avert it. While the inaugural address was being delivered from this place, devoted altogether to saving the Union without war, insurgent agents were in the city seeking to *destroy* it without war—seeking to dissolve the Union, and divide effects, by negotiation. Both parties deprecated war; but one of them would *make* war rather than let the nation survive; and the other would *accept* war rather than let it perish. And the war came.
One eighth of the whole population were colored slaves, not distributed generally over the Union, but localized in the southern part of it. These slaves constituted a peculiar and powerful interest. All knew that this interest was, somehow, the cause of the war. To strengthen, perpetuate, and extend this interest was the object for which the insurgents would rend the Union, even by war; while the government claimed no right to do more than to restrict the territorial enlargement of it. Neither party

22

This scene at Lincoln's second Inaugural March 4, 1865 is attributed to the photographer Alexander Gardner.

expected for the war, the magnitude, or the duration, which it has already attained. Neither anticipated that the *cause* of the conflict might cease with, or even before, the conflict itself should cease. Each looked for an easier triumph, and a result less fundamental and astounding. Both read the same Bible, and pray to the same God; and each invokes His aid against the other. It may seem strange that any men should dare to ask a just God's assistance in wringing their bread from the sweat of other men's faces; but let us judge not that we be not judged. The prayers of both could not be answered; that of neither has been answered fully. The Almighty has His own purposes. "Woe unto the world because of offences! for it must needs be that offences come; but woe to that man by whom the offence cometh!" If we shall suppose that American slavery is one of those offences which, in the providence of God, must needs come, but which, having continued through His appointed time, He now wills to remove, and that He gives to both North and South, this terrible war, as the woe due to those by whom the offence came, shall we discern therein any departure from those divine attributes which the believers in a Living God always ascribe to Him? Fondly do we hope—fervently do we pray—that this mighty scourge of war may speedily pass away. Yet, if God wills that it continue, until all the wealth piled by the bondman's two hundred and fifty years of unrequited toil shall be sunk, and until every drop of blood drawn with the lash, shall be paid by another drawn with the sword, as was said three thousand years ago, so still it must be said "the judgments of the Lord are true and righteous altogether."

With malice toward none; with charity for all; with firmness in the right, as God gives us to see the right, let us strive on to finish the work we are in; to bind up the nation's wounds; to care for him who shall have borne the battle, and for his widow, and his orphan—to do all which may achieve and cherish a just, and a lasting peace, among ourselves, and with all nations.

23

On April fourth, Lincoln, with Admiral Porter and a guard of sailors, inspected evacuated Richmond. Five days later Lee surrendered to Grant at Appomattox. On the evening of the fourteenth the actor John Wilkes Booth entered the President's box at Ford's Theatre and shot the President in the head. Leaping from the box to the stage, he waved a knife and yelled "Sic semper tyrannis!" and ran past the actors off the stage into the night. The President was carried unconscious to a rooming house across the street where he died shortly after seven the next morning. His funeral was

The caption for this famous sketch in *Leslie's* (May 6, 1865) read: "Assassination of President Lincoln—the murderer leaping upon the stage, and catching his spur in the flag which hung before the President's box—from a sketch by our special artist Albert Berghaus."

There were many such processions as this during Lincoln's funeral. Here the hearse is passing under the arch at 12th Street, in Chicago, Illinois, in May 1865. The photograph was taken by S. Fassett.

extraordinary and moving. As the train carrying his body moved slowly westward, people from the towns and the farms all the way to Springfield stood beside the tracks, crying.

Portrait of Mrs. Lincoln at the age of forty-three, dressed for a formal occasion, taken by Mathew Brady in Washington in 1861. The original is in the Ostendorf collection.

THE ELECTED WIFE

It is certain that we Americans hope that each man elected President will prove to be great. If he appears a little less than wise in foreign affairs, or delegates too much of the work to another, or is not faultless in manners, he is marked down in greatness. We are told again and again that we engage in a personality cult when we ought to measure a President by his policies. Nothing is likely to change the personality cult, especially since the camera cult hardly makes a thousand pictures atone for one page of thought. Therefore we accept the fact that an American President has the misfortune to stand in a personal relationship to each American, to be loved, hated, defended like a man's own honor, or fiercely scolded, even destroyed. What then is the fortune of his immediate relatives, the wife and children and any others who go along with the furniture to the presidential mansion? They too live with each American family for a time, and on a first-name basis.

More than any member of his family, the President's wife becomes as much the property of the people as if she too was elected. She is so intensely liked or disliked, examined and discussed, that she too eventually receives a grade in greatness. A few of them have declined the role and literally retreated to an upstairs room in the White House. In recent years some have modeled the role successfully under the directing skill of those on the executive staff who understood protocol and the protection of First Ladies. Many have been remarkable women in their own right. Of the thirty-seven wives of Presidents—not all of whom lived through a presidential experience—a good dozen are worth admiring and a few more are worth investigating because of the gossip that trails their memory.

The people of the past are alive in the people of today if we accept the idea that human nature is much the same, century in and century out. Under the hoary names of John and Abigail Adams lies a romantic love more intense and frank than a modern fiction writer would dare imagine. Martha Washington and Dolley Madison are celebrated enough in literature, but what a literature! It is almost as if they were second-rate characters for whom cheap sentimentality sufficed. Yet if the tradition of Virginia plantation civilization is worth paying attention to, Martha is one of its handsomest

27

examples; while Dolley would be unique and vital in any age. Then there are slighter figures but interesting ones, such as Jefferson's Martha, not much more than a ghost but the heart of his youth and most productive years, and Jackson's Rachel, whom he loved like a knight of old and lost amid the bitter calumny of the politicians. Pallid John Tyler was a heartier man in his family than in politics, had two wives and fifteen children, of whom many survived him, the last dying during President Truman's administration. Franklin Pierce, equally ineffectual in politics, had a disastrous family life both because of the loss of his children and the morbid retreat of his delicate wife. Lucy Polk, wife of the empire builder, was a quiet but stubborn puritan, while Lucy Hayes set a style for crusading piety, but both were concerned with the moral rather than the social responsibilities of the White House.

Not the least of all the heroines must be the sixteen-year-old girl who married and educated Andrew Johnson, and, in a sense, a heroine of tragedy was Mary Todd Lincoln, whose whole story has only recently been told. Cleveland's White House bride, young, pretty and vastly inexperienced, had to survive the rugged education of public life that began with her honeymoon and did so nobly, to become one of the pleasantest figures of a First Lady absorbed entirely in the personal life of a great man. Against her example of competence the pathetic efforts of McKinley's beloved Ida show the horrors of a sickly woman thrust into that position.

With the turn of the nineteenth century, "old-fashioned wife" became a phrase indicating that women were beginning to have a choice in the married state. Edith Roosevelt had the mind and character to exert influence over brilliant and sometimes volatile Teddy. In his strong-minded family she not only made a place for herself and presided calmly over a lively brood of young Roosevelts, but became the dominant feminine factor in his life in spite of the haunting memory of the wife of his youth. The Roosevelts, with their energy in every direction and their cosmopolitan social tastes, gave the White House a glamor that enchanted the nation. Not for a day could Americans take their eyes off the doings of the Roosevelts, and ever since, in spite of some discouraging occupants, they have looked in happy expectation to the

White House for front-page stories as well as a gloss of beauty in American life.

In recent years some First Ladies, such as Lou Henry Hoover and the less original Grace Coolidge, conscious of what is expected of them, have chosen to create a formal image of themselves as creatures of patrician but smiling dignity in beautiful, flowing gowns. But there was Bess Truman, who declined to become stylized and kept her sense of humor in spite of the flattery of those about her who meant well but might have turned her head. It is true that the White House style ill became ambitious Florence Harding, whose personal standards were no more edifying than those of her husband. She, however, was part of a grim period in the presidency, and like her Warren was a victim of cynical politics.

A different accident of politics forced on Wilson's second wife an importance she never sought, placing a woman for the first time in a position of presidential responsibility. Less dramatic and not played on the front of the stage was the undoubtedly important role of Eleanor Roosevelt as roving sub-President and adviser. It is possible that she because of her independent career as a humane and inspirational public figure had helped to lift the part of the First Lady out of the disputes of politics. Though it is dangerous to generalize, especially about such an illusory phenomenon as public opinion, in recent years there seems to appear in the newspapers more intelligent understanding of the women elected by accident to stand under the presidential floodlights. Even the bitterest critics of Franklin D. Roosevelt came in time to agree that Eleanor was a great credit to her country.

Possibly the White House is today a protection as well as a test of quality. We Americans may be coming around to looking for what we can like in a First Lady, so long as it does not interfere with the full enjoyment of our partisan opinions. Jacqueline Kennedy, even before her husband's assassination, enjoyed something of a non-partisan popularity. Perhaps this is because she is that rarest creature, a woman who creates the inspiring illusion of a great beauty. Ladybird Johnson, who had against her the snob prejudices of the East, in a remarkably short time established a respectable position for herself. If the tempering process of the presidency refines a prosaic politician into a statesman, it is not impossible that in these days of educated women a First Lady will be able to fulfill the role that Americans somewhat optimistically assign her.

More Presidents have been closely bound in marriage than one would expect to find among the ordinary run of husbands. Whether this is chance or the workings of the ancient political cliche that no divorced man can be President, the domestic life of the White House has generally been exemplary. Only one President, Buchanan, was a bachelor, and besides Jefferson and Jackson, only three did not have the company of their wives during their presidency. Van Buren's wife died early, before he became a national figure. William Henry Harrison's wife did not accompany him to Washington and never joined him during his thirty-two day administration, and Arthur's wife died nearly two years before he succeeded to the presidency on Garfield's assassination.

Most of the presidential families were well supplied with children, who added interest to the news of the executive mansion. They were inevitably spoiled by public attention when they were young enough to be susceptible to it. Otherwise, they presented the usual excitement, comforts, and problems of children. There was one who matched the brilliance of his father, a few who were tragic weaklings, but mostly they were not remarkable and their passage through the public view was short. They were the family climate of a public man, nothing more. Only two of these men had a dynastic importance in politics, John Adams and Theodore Roosevelt. Like their genealogy, social and economic background, the Presidents' progeny belonged to the stream of democratic life, and except for a natural pride in being "descended," their descendents have gone quietly about their business, usually without much fame.

Such is also true of the wives who survived Presidents, except for a few striking exceptions. Nevertheless, having once worn, figuratively, the diadem, a touch of glory remained to them for all their lives, and in the pages of history they continue to be figures of interest, speculation, and even importance.

MARY ANN TODD LINCOLN

Robert Smith Todd, grocer, banker, cotton manufacturer, lawyer, and perennial clerk of the Kentucky House of Representatives, was a fair example of a successful gentleman in the formative years of the American nation. Besides his preoccupation with paying enterprise and politics, he married twice and managed to rear thirteen children with a great deal of care and tenderness. There were five by his first wife, Eliza Ann Parker, and eight by his second, Elizabeth Humphreys. Perhaps the most fascinating and gifted was Mary Ann, generally called Molly, third daughter of the first brood, who was destined to go down in history as the wife of Abraham Lincoln. The Todds were fortunate in that they lived in Lexington, a small town then but already the state capital, prospering market town of the Blue Grass Country, and, as it liked to think, home of all that was civilized and gracious on the western frontier.

Molly was born on December 13, 1818, into a family not only large but clannish in its loyalties. Her first major misery came, when she was seven, with the death of her mother, who succumbed to the uncertainties of childbirth, taking the baby with her. Robert Todd married again sixteen months later, selecting a Virginian who brought with her some strange notions about the ascendancy of the aristocracy, of which she fancied herself a member, and began to whip her stepchildren into shape as little aristocrats. Molly, being at best a headstrong child and not easy to manage, had no hope of accommodating herself to the idea of her own mother's brisk replacement, much less the discipline of a strict stepmother. Fortunately she had the companionship of her two older sisters, Lizzie and Frances, to cushion her resentment.

School for Robert Todd's bright little Molly meant Dr. John Ward's Academy. This schoolmaster had evolved the theory that brains work best early in the morning. Consequently he began school at dawn and the children were

This daguerreotype of Mary Lincoln was made by Nicholas Shepherd at about the same time he did the one of Lincoln. It was taken four years after her marriage, and according to the unpublished memoirs of a part-time servant, Mariah Vance, Mary dusted off the two portraits in the Springfield house parlor one day and observed, "They are very precious to me, taken when we were young and so desperately in love. They will grace the walls of the White House." Lincoln, who was standing beside her, laughed and remarked, "I trust that that grace never slips a peg and becomes dis-grace." (Quoted from *Lincoln in Photographs,* by Charles Hamilton and Lloyd Ostendorf.)

obliged to fumble their way through half-dark streets to arrive on time. When she was ready to progress to higher learning at fourteen, a semi-boarding arrangement was made for her with

Madame Victorie Charlotte Leclerc Mentelle, by which she lived at school during the week and at home over weekends. Mme Mentelle's establishment was a finishing school in the truest sense of the phrase, for she claimed to turn out young ladies with the manners and accomplishments of the best French tradition. The curriculum bore heavily on the French language and the art of dancing. It was a gambol for Molly from beginning to end, and she spent four gloriously happy years there. Following graduation she paid a visit to Springfield, Illinois, where both of her older sisters were settling down, Lizzie married, and Frances about to be married. Lizzie's husband was Ninian Edwards, a prominent young lawyer and, as it happened, a political friend of Abraham Lincoln.

Though Molly Todd returned to Lexington and resumed her education under the guidance of her old teacher, Dr. Ward, she was restless, both because a girl of her breeding must be thinking of marriage and because she was still not comfortable with her stepmother. So two years later, in 1839, she returned to Lizzie's Springfield home for good. She was then twenty, a fresh-faced little girl with rosy cheeks and brown hair, clever and vivacious. She liked to flirt but was often tempted to dazzle the men and could never gauge the effect of her cleverness or her exceedingly candid opinions. Nevertheless she was a shining addition to Springfield society, which, of course, in those rustic days was a somewhat limited affair. Sister Lizzie Edwards took her own social position seriously and doubtless expected Molly to find a husband from the field of young men of approximately the same status. When the girl responded to the attentions of poor, ill-bred Abe Lincoln she was surprised. As the couple progressed to the point of becoming engaged, late in 1840, her feeling that they were ill-assorted for marriage was made clear to Molly, but without making the slightest impression, it seemed.

The truth is Molly gravitated invariably to the strong-minded, positive person, perhaps because she admired so much the mental ruggedness that had been left out of her own chemistry. She was a woman all feeling and impulse, incapable of scheming to catch a husband. Nevertheless Abe

33

broke the engagement, in a fog of doubt as to the sufficiency of love in the match, particularly on his part. Molly released him with such understanding and sweetness, that there was some doubt among her friends as to who had jilted whom. She continued to be busy and gay socially, while Abe worried so about his part in the affair that he made himself ill. The engagement was broken in January of 1841, and the couple did not see each other again for more than a year and a half. Molly had plenty of time to turn to another suitor, and she did occasionally pair off with a rising young Springfield politician, Stephen A. Douglas, but nothing came of it. Then Lincoln became involved in one of those serio-comic incidents that were not uncommon in his young years.

The Whig *Sangamo Journal* published a series of letters, all signed by fictitious names, ridiculing an uppish Democrat named James Shields. Lincoln contributed two, and Molly in collaboration with a girl friend, one. While Lincoln's were light and folksy, Molly's thrusts were so sharp that Shields was furious and, guessing the author, told Lincoln that he intended to do something about what he thought an outrageous personal attack. In order to save Molly embarrassment, Lincoln told Shields it was he who wrote the letter. Whereupon Shields challenged him to a duel. Pondering this unforeseen predicament Abe, having choice of weapons, decided that the least dangerous encounter he could think of would be one with broadswords. Since he was tall and Shields very short, the advantage would be with him. So on the appointed day angry little Shields and lanky, worried Lincoln faced each other on the field of honor equipped with broadswords. Before the duel could begin, however, Shields calmed down and accepted an apology, so it was called off, much to Lincoln's satisfaction.

The affair brought Molly and Abe together again. Discreetly they began seeing each other at the house of friends. Their marriage, on November 4, 1842, was arranged at the last moment, with about twenty-five friends hastily assembled at the Ninian Edwards's house for the ceremony and wedding supper. Psychologically, both bride and groom were well prepared for marriage, that is, each had seen enough of it in their friends to decide that it was a desirable state, and they had proved their mutual affection by coming back together after a long separation of their own making.

Lincoln was so poor and so encumbered with debt from his Salem days that he was obliged to install his finely bred Kentucky bride in mean accommodations at a boardinghouse called the Globe Tavern. Then he was obliged to leave her alone for long stretches when he was away following the court circuit. Fortunately he was able to buy a house the following year, 1844, of one and a half stories at the corner of Eighth and Jackson streets in Springfield, the same house, later raised to two stories, that is now the historic Lincoln Homestead.

Robert Todd, in Lexington, took note of his son-in-law's meager finances and contributed to them regularly for several years, until Lincoln's professional income rose to a sufficiency. Rise it did after marriage, as Lincoln reversed his casual attitude toward the procedures and precedents of the law and knuckled down to studying his profession as he never had before. Molly, for her part, undertook the responsibilities and drudgery of a poor man's household with a good will. She cooked, baked, cleaned, sewed, and she relentlessly tried to tidy up the appearance and habits of a husband who had never in his life been disciplined by a regular household. Her own breeding, her pride in good appearances, and the challenge of two wealthy sisters in town, impelled her to toil beyond her physical strength for her home. She developed migraine headaches and occasionally collapsed into fits of hysterical bad temper, at which times anyone within range including her husband, would try to move out of range until good humor was restored.

By and large the Lincolns had far more good times together than bad. Molly was gay and loved company, fond, perhaps overfond, of the children born to her, and an equally fond wife. Lincoln's tenderness encompassed both his wife and his children. He seldom lost patience with the former and was a delighted playfellow of the latter, holding to the belief that they should be allowed to grow as nature intended without force or discipline. He fully understood the compulsions of Molly's emotional temperament, and as to her bursts of temper, argued that "it does her lots of good and it doesn't hurt me a bit."

35

Their first child's birth was on August 1, 1843. He was named Robert Todd, grew up the quietest member of the family, the only one to reach his majority, and succeeded in having a career above the average—Secretary of War by Garfield's appointment, Minister to Great Britain under Benjamin Harrison, and later president of the Pullman Company. Edward Baker, born March 10, 1846, did not live past his fourth year. It was Bob and Eddie who went to Washington and spent a season at Mrs. Spriggs's boardinghouse when Lincoln served a term in the House of Representatives. Eddie died on February 1, 1850, and at the end of that year, on December 21st, a third boy, William Wallace, was born, the child said to have some of his father's charm, who was to die in the White House. The youngest, Thomas Wallace, nicknamed Tad for tadpole by Lincoln because as a baby his head was too big for his body, was born on April 4, 1853.

From the birth of Bob, Lincoln called Molly "Mother," while she, with a touch of Victorian formality, continued to call him "Mr. Lincoln." The children, shaggy country boys in the clothes their mother made for them, called their parents "Maw" and "Paw." Surely there was nothing remarkable about the Lincoln family. Other wives were ambitious for their husbands and nagged them to get on in the world. It was not unheard of, even in a border town like Springfield, for the mistress of a household to make up her invitation lists from "the best people" and blackball those not the best. If Mary Lincoln had her worldly side, she was also a staunch churchwoman and personal friend of her Presbyterian pastor, Dr. James Smith, who, she constantly hoped, would bring Mr. Lincoln to an acceptance of religion. She was also impulsively warmhearted and could be counted on for all the kindnesses of a good neighbor. For instance, there was the time, shortly after Tad was born, when she nursed another woman's baby with her own because the mother was ill, and regularly sent Mr. Lincoln to pick up and return the child.

Certain frailties she had. Thunderstorms terrified her, and the approach of one would send Mr. Lincoln hurrying home to hold her hand. When it came to money, she was hopelessly impractical, swinging from miserliness to ex-

Although Lincoln himself never joined any church, he did attend the First Presbyterian Church in Springfield, Illinois. Mary Lincoln was a member and their son Tad was baptized there. In those days, families paid a pew fee instead of making a pledge to support the church. Lincoln paid his fee regularly and occupied the left half of the pew shown above. Today it stands in the sanctuary of the First Presbyterian Church at Seventh and Capitol streets. Tad and Mrs. Lincoln were buried from this building.

travagance. Her most costly weakness was strong opinions about people, often freely and sharply expressed. She did not like the young man Lincoln had taken into his office as junior partner because she had decided that his manners were rough, that he drank too much, and that he was an infidel. She refused to invite him ever to dinner. The young man, Billy Herndon, was sorely hurt by the snub, and many years later, after Lincoln's death, returned the favor with interest. As a prime source of material on Lincoln and his family, he was able to put into circulation a picture of Mary Lincoln distorted by his prejudice, one that caused her much pain and also did the cause of dispassionate history no good.

An interesting question about Mary Todd Lincoln that has never been given the speculation it deserves is what part she may have played in Lincoln's career. It is known that she

37

was bright, articulate, and interested in politics. Her father was political and so was Lexington, for many reasons, including the majestic influence of its first citizen Henry Clay. Without this pro-politics bias, she might have persuaded Lincoln to concentrate on law and make money. She never did. Once, it is known, she made the decision for him on a major move. It was after he had left Congress, when, discouraged by a sense of failure, he was tempted to accept an appointment as governor of the New Oregon Territory. Mary was against it and persuaded him to turn it down. Thus he returned to Springfield, his law practice, and the decade that led to the presidency.

During that decade of the fifties it is likely that Lincoln discussed his evolving philosophy on the slavery question at home. Molly had a keen mind and could stand up to him in argument. She also had an incurable fancy for literary composition. So it is probable that he honed his ideas and the highly tempered simplicity of his English on her criticism. At any rate, she gave him plenty of room to pursue his own course, suggesting that she was a wife of some understanding and generosity, for his course had its meanders and the prospect of its getting him anywhere was not always clear. When, in fact, the presidency was his, her satisfaction was immeasurable.

To Mary Lincoln the prospect of becoming mistress of the White House was heady stuff. She understood that the woman she would succeed, Buchanan's niece Harriet Lane, was a great lady, with a European polish, also that Washington was full of social snobs who would expect Mrs. Lincoln to be nothing better than a country bumpkin. Proud and apprehensive, Molly decided to go to New York and buy a proper wardrobe. When she got there in January and discovered that dressmakers, jewelers, and all the purveyors of feminine finery would give her any amount of credit, she bought extravagantly. This was the first tally in her debts for clothes and adornments that were to amount in the next four years to a sum that she had no hope of paying. Lincoln had no suspicion of what she was up to. Certainly the cost of women's clothes, and even his wife's inner fears of the rôle she was

Mrs. Lincoln with Willie and Tad, taken in Springfield in 1860 by Preston Butler.

called on to play, were matters he thought little of as he made his own preparations for Washington.

It was decided that Lincoln's journey to his inaugural would be in the nature of a political demonstration. His train would take a leisurely course and he would make back-platform appearances all along the way, stop over for receptions here and there, and meet the leaders of the Republican party. It would be a twelve-day trip, crowded, noisy, and tiring. Therefore he would take with him his aides, some political friends, and of his family only Bob, the oldest boy, then a freshman at Harvard. Mary and the two little ones

Robert Todd Lincoln, as he looked in 1864.

would follow by regular passenger train. However, the more Mary learned of the preparations for the presidential excursion, the less she could bear to miss it. At the last

40

moment Lincoln yielded to her wishes and took the whole family with him.

It was an unforgettable journey. Among the bright young men of the party were John Nicolay, presidential secretary, and his assistant John Hay. Ward Lamon, Lincoln's old friend and partner, came along with his guitar and his repertory of Negro songs. Mary's favorite was a gallant young aide named Elmer Ellsworth, who four months later was to become a Civil War Hero by giving his life to haul down a Confederate flag flaunted from a house in Alexandria, Virginia. Mary behaved with dignity, remaining entirely in the background. Sometimes the crowds at the train stops caught sight of her sitting behind a window, when they would wave and she would smile and flutter a hand in response. The two younger boys, Willie and Tad, untamed imps of ten and seven, amused themselves by scrambling off the train as soon as it stopped and running through the crowds, from which they had to be extricated before the train could move on. The President-elect's own car was a wonder of luxury, brand new and especially designed. On the outside, its orange panels picked out with brown scrolls, declared that this was *the* car. Inside, it had a thick carpet in tapestry pattern, polished woods, and side walls of crimson plush, and blue silk curtains, on which were exactly thirty-four silver stars, the number of the states in—and out—of the Union.

All went well until the last stage, from Philadelphia to Washington, when a detective in the employ of the Philadelphia, Wilmington & Baltimore Railway, Allan Pinkerton, came aboard with a story that there was a plot to attack Lincoln as he changed trains in Baltimore. Lincoln was not impressed, but most of his party were frightened. Baltimore was a "southern" town and one might expect any violence from southern detestation of Lincoln. There had been constant threats from the South against Lincoln, and one addressed to Mary Lincoln had been particularly grisly. Someone, in South Carolina it seemed, sent her a painting showing Lincoln tarred and feathered, his ankles chained and a rope about his neck. Pinkerton, who was always self-assured and plausible, proposed to take Lincoln off the train and

41

hustle him secretly through Baltimore. Against his judgment, Lincoln agreed, and so, while his family and suite continued on as planned, he hurried ahead, arriving in Washington before the news that he had left the train was out.

Mary Lincoln, whose terror for her husband's safety, and her own, was always near the surface, went through this trial with unaccustomed courage. There was no attack, and the

Lincoln's "disguise" at Baltimore became the subject for many caricatures such as this one by Aldalbert Volck, showing Lincoln in a Scotch cap and military cloak. Mr. Shaw reports the historian Benson Lossing as quoting Lincoln about the clothes he wore that gave rise to the story. "In New York some friend had given me a new beaver hat in a box, and in it had placed a soft wool hat. I had never worn one of the latter in my life. I had this box in my room. Having informed a very few friends of the secret of my new movements, and the cause, I put on an old overcoat that I had with me, and putting the soft hat in my pocket, I walked out of the house at a back door, bareheaded, without exciting any special curiosity. Then I put on the soft hat and joined my friends without being recognized by strangers, for I was not the same man." Ward Hill Lamon traveled with him. Lincoln did not believe that there was actual danger in Baltimore, but thought it wiser to run no risk.

family was happily re-united at Willard's Hotel in Washington. The Capital was an uneasy, changing town. Much of the southern element was packing its carriages and rattling off across the Potomac, while from the north dusty militiamen marched in to camp on the White House lawn and patrol Pennsylvania Avenue. Nevertheless the usual inaugural ceremonies were ordered. There was a ball, at which Mrs. Lincoln, the focus of all curiosity, looked charming in a billowing blue dress cut low in the bodice to show her pretty white shoulders, with a wreath of flowers clasping her smooth brown hair. Since the President did not dance, she led off the

Mrs. Lincoln in a ball gown typical of those she liked to wear, and with flowers in her hair. Taken by Mathew Brady in 1861.

ball with Stephen A. Douglas, the defeated northern Democratic presidential candidate and her girlhood beau. A considerable delegation of Todd relatives were there, having trooped up loyally from Lexington, though the family was Confederate in sympathy.

By the standards of fashion and society Mary Lincoln handled herself superbly in Washington. After two years, so

43

eminent a journalist as Perley Poore had nothing but praise for her and pronounced her the best fitted "by nature and by education" of all the White House hostesses since Mrs. Madison. That she proceeded with a full schedule of public and private entertainments during her first year, regardless of the Civil War, was not so remarkable at that time, since most of the North was lethargic in sacrificing habits of peace. When some of the Lincoln opposition found it "heartless," she remarked philosophically that she would be equally criticized for not entertaining. The obligations of her position, she was determined, would be fully met, and she even undertook to shake hands with the thousands who flocked to her public receptions, until her tiny hand was in such a painful state that she gave that up and bowed instead.

Private visitors, even those who had not expected to like her, often departed as her warm friends and defenders, for in personal contact she had a winning way with people. She made many friends in Washington, including such surprising ones as stern Secretary of War Stanton and the equally formidable abolitionist senator from Massachusetts, Charles Sumner. Her devoted companion, particularly when she was ill or in distress, was an ardent champion of the Negro cause, Lizzie Keckley, a mulatto and former slave who first came to the White House as a seamstress.

The general public was little aware of Mary Lincoln's personal charms; on the contrary, it treated her to more personal abuse than any President's wife before Eleanor Roosevelt. The reason was simple and beyond her control. She happened to be a Todd of Kentucky, and during the Civil War the Todds were Confederates, many of their men serving, and dying, on that side. It was easy to think she was pro-Confederate at heart. Her style, her gaiety was "southern," and people believed what they wanted to believe. Even the President's secretary, bright but opinionated John Hay, detested the Todds and privately nicknamed Mrs. Lincoln "The Enemy." The public never knew that she was thoroughly indoctrinated in the Lincoln philosophy, that she was by nature an emotionally partisan wife, that, though sometimes as indiscreet as a schoolgirl where her sentiments

The Lincoln family in 1861, a lithograph engraved by J.C. Buttre in 1878 from a painting by Francis B. Carpenter, showing Mary, Willie, and Robert, and Tad with Abraham Lincoln. There is no known photograph of the Lincoln family for which they posed as a whole. Carpenter used a favorite Brady photograph of Tad with his father and whatever photographs he could find of individual members of the family for his models.

were involved, her relations with her family were set aside for the war's duration.

Toward the end of the third year of war, a Todd did actually reach the White House, by a typically Lincolnian act of mercy. Mary's half-sister Emilie Todd Helm—"Little Sister," Lincoln called her—after the death of her husband in the Confederate Army, was detained at Fort Munroe when she tried to get passage through Union lines and return with her little daughter to Lexington. Lincoln directed that she be sent to Washington, where she visited a little while and noted in her diary that the President was worried about his wife's mental condition. The public pressures and private woes apparently threatened a complete nervous breakdown.

As to the public pressures, Mrs. Lincoln had assumed from the very beginning a resistant attitude. "My character is wholly domestic and the public have nothing to do with it,"

Mrs. Lincoln in mourning after
the death of Willie

Photograph of William Wallace Lincoln
(1850-1862) taken in Washington, D.C., in
1861 by Mathew B. Brady

46

she said. The loose charges that she was a Confederate spy she refused to dignify with an answer. Nevertheless she protected herself against the vile abuse that loaded her mail by having an aide cull it of the mud-slinging letters before it was brought to her. And her character became so much a public issue that the President was impelled to say to Congress that he guaranteed his wife's loyalty. Still, she weathered the political mischances of the presidency fairly well; her personal difficulties and misfortunes were the factors that threatened to unbalance her. Her irresponsibility with money entangled her almost at once. Having secured $20,000 from Congress to spruce up the White House, which struck her as disgracefully shabby, before she was through with the new brocades, decoration and trimmings, she had spent $6,700 more than Congress had appropriated. Since this was public money, the President had to find out about it, and for once he was thoroughly angry with his wife, scolding her for buying "flub-dubs for this damned old house, when the soldiers cannot have blankets." Eventually Congress paid the bills, to save Lincoln from going into his own pocket. White House running expenses threatened to involve her in an even more serious scandal, when she placed her confidence in the obliging head gardener, one Major Watt, who, it appeared, juggled the books in her interest. Before he could be dismissed, Lincoln was obliged to pay him $1,500 for three notes Mary had written him. She was ashamed of the embarrassment caused by her blunder, but somehow felt more keenly Watt's betrayal of her confidence.

The disaster that truly haunted Mary Lincoln in the White House was the death of Willie of a "bilious fever"—perhaps typhoid—on February 20, 1862. It was feared that she would never stop weeping and grieving. She was ill with sorrow, requiring a nurse, while the fourth of the boys, Tad, added to her anxiety by having a long siege of the same disease as Willie. It was a matter of months before she could resume the simple routine of necessary duties, the mail, the daily round of visits to the wounded in the army hospitals, a few visitors. All White House entertaining had been stopped, even the Marine Band concerts on the White House lawn. The President's wife was seen in nothing but black from then on. She avoided anything that reminded her of the dead boy, his bedroom, and even the room where he had been prepared for burial, yet she slipped away to visit a spiritualist. When Lincoln had him exposed as a fake, she turned to another.

The following summer, the President moved his family from the heat and smells of Washington to the Soldier's Home, on a slight elevation at the edge of town, an easy drive from the White House. On such a drive in 1863, Mary Lincoln was painfully hurt when her driver's seat broke loose, pitching him into the ditch, and starting the horses on a wild run, and a minute later she too was flung from the carriage, striking the back of her head on a rock. The wound kept her in bed several weeks, but she was able to take her physical ills cheerfully, and this was one of the good months of the war, when the Confederate Army had been turned back at Gettysburg. The psychological ills, however, gave her no rest. Though she was protected from further difficulties with the mysteries of official moneys, she was unable to control her own compulsive buying, and her secret debt grew steadily. Undoubtedly she never faced its figure, which eventually added up to some $29,000. But she was obliged to face the possibility that after the 1864 election she would be the President's wife no longer, and the dressmakers would crowd in on her for payment. This fear, fed on Lincoln's own pessimism about his re-election, haunted her most of that year. Emotionally she clung to the stalwart kindness of her husband, who as the President had little time for her and had to exert immense patience not to treat her as a nuisance.

As the second Lincoln inaugural approached, the White House family was sad and shriveled. Bob was in Virginia, serving on Grant's staff. Tad was a lonely little boy, without Willie. Gone was the mischief and the fun of such enterprises as selling gingerbread and candy to the office seekers who came through the front door. He took to dogging his father's heels, being allowed to do as he pleased, even to playing in the presidential office when his father was there working, no matter what momentous business was in hand nor how long the hours were. Often, late in the evening, he fell asleep in

This photograph of Tad with his father is one of five poses taken by Alexander Gardner on April 10, 1865, just four days before Lincoln was assassinated. As so often in photographic studios in those days, a fancy backdrop has been added to the original.

some corner of the office and was carried off to bed by his father.

With the fall of Petersburg and Richmond on April 2, 1865, the time for the North to unfurl its flags and celebrate arrived. Mary Lincoln drove south in an army ambulance to join the President for a grand review of the victorious forces at City Point. It was a rough, jouncing trip and she arrived too late to sit a horse and take the review at his side. When she saw that the commanding general's wife, beautiful Mrs. Ord, had taken her place, her nerves snapped and she launched such angry remarks at the lady and the President as should have issued only from the lips of a jealous virago. It was a very public scene, one that humiliated her acutely in retrospect, and on an excuse of being ill she returned to Washington to recover her equilibrium. In a few days she returned with an official party, on the *River Queen*, to inspect Petersburg and return with Lincoln to Washington on the 9th, the day of Lee's surrender at Appomattox.

Washington had a great illumination and victory celebration two days later, and on the 14th the Lincolns and a young couple went to Ford's Theatre to enjoy a popular comedy. Mary was sitting close to her husband, holding his hand, when John Wilkes Booth slipped into the presidential box and shot the President. She screamed and fainted. When she was brought back to consciousness, the dying President had been taken across the street to Peterson's boardinghouse, and she was taken to his bedside. All during the harrowing hours of that night, the most pitiable sight was her hysterical grief. She clung to her unconscious husband, kissing him passionately again and again, begging him to speak to her, begging him not to die or to take her with him in death. Several times she was led from the room, only to insist on returning. It was some time after the President was pronounced dead in the gray morning hours that she could be led weeping and moaning to a carriage and taken to the White House, where she was put to bed and lay ill all during the funeral, the return of Lincoln's body to Springfield, and for many days afterward.

Five weeks later, the President's widow was a woeful little woman driving to the station for her journey westward.

50

She had decided not to return to Springfield but to go to Chicago. Congress had given her a year's presidential salary, and with this she bought a house, only to realize that she was without means to live in it. Lincoln's estate of $87,000 when it was settled, would be divided into three parts among his immediate heirs, since he died without a will. In the meantime, she not only was without income, she faced her dressmakers' bills. Inevitably, it occurred to her that she could raise money on her White House finery. There was a lot of it, in fact such a mountain of it when packed to be moved, that evil people had started the rumor that some of the White House furnishings were hidden in the hoopskirts. Traveling to New York with Lizzie Keckley as companion, she approached a commission broker incognito, with some jewelry for sale. The gentleman at Brady & Co. was clever enough to penetrate her disguise and try to make a good thing of the lady's distress.

A hopeless innocent in business matters, Mary Lincoln entrusted him with letters to certain politicians, who, in her confused way, she believed had a moral obligation to pay her debts. The broker was to act as her agent in attempting to persuade them to do so. When this had failed, Brady & Co. persuaded her to agree to a public sale of her clothes and jewelry, and to her astonishment used these letters to give it publicity. The publicity naturally was sensational, and Mary, once more feeling betrayed by those she had trusted, withdrew from the project bitterly humiliated. Eventually she paid $800 to recover her belongings.

Senator Sumner tried to urge through Congress a pension for Lincoln's widow, finally secured $3,000 a year for her, after five years' effort, instead of the $5,000 asked. She was not to be allowed, for many years, to withdraw into the peace of obscurity. No sooner was the dress scandal forgotten than book publishers began to bring her back into the limelight. The first publication, in 1868, was by her companion and friend Lizzie Keckley, who was persuaded to tell all under the title *Behind the Scenes,* in the belief that she was presenting a defense of her former mistress. It had a great sale as a controversial book, but was not at all what Mary Lincoln felt she needed; consequently Mrs. Keckley was added to the list of those who had betrayed her confidence. Longing for peace,

Mrs. Lincoln decided to go to Europe and live amongst strangers, so as soon as Bob's long-planned marriage to Senator Harlan's daughter Mary was accomplished in September of that year, she set out with Tad for Frankfurt in Germany. It was almost three years before she returned, bringing her boy home to die of a lung ailment, presumably tuberculosis, in Chicago on July 15, 1871.

The following year Ward Lamon's *The Life of Abraham Lincoln*, ghost-written by Chauncey F. Black from material supplied by her old enemy Billy Herndon, seemed so grossly unfair, not to say scandalous, that Mary thought fit to denounce it publicly. Not long afterward she tangled directly with Herndon over a lecture he delivered, in which he rationalized Lincoln as an agnostic after his own pattern. As a religious woman, she was deeply shocked and took issue with him, showing that the old, disputatious spirit was still alive. To her he responded coldly with a broadside calling her a liar and a madwoman. She was, in fact, a woeful soul, traveling aimlessly, suffering hallucinations, sometimes spending wildly, sometimes obsessed with the fear of poverty. Robert Lincoln, thinking she had deteriorated to the point of being unable to look after herself, decided to have her declared legally incompetent so that she could be looked after.

The law required that Mary Todd Lincoln be tried before a jury for insanity. This for her was the final abyss of humiliation, and when the court pronounced her insane, she tried to commit suicide. Prevented from taking poison, she was taken to Dr. R. J. Patterson's sanitarium in Batavia, Illinois, where she received the psychiatric treatment she had so long needed. She improved so rapidly that she was allowed to move to her sister Lizzie Edwards s home in Springfield. There she concentrated all her thought on a campaign to have the insanity verdict reversed, and on June 15, 1876, another court, in Chicago, agreed that she was legally sane and released her from custody. One of her first acts upon this triumph was to write Robert and demand that he return all of her property that he had stolen. Then she went to France to live.

Finally, she was allowed to be forgotten. She traveled a little, a lonely mousey woman in black, living in cheap hotels

52

for four years, until, having become semi-paralyzed from a fall off a ladder, she returned to the United States, in October 1880. Congress was now in a more generous mood and raised her pension to $5,000, allowing her besides $15,000 for medical expenses. After the doctors in New York had done what they could for her, she returned to Lizzie's house and lived out the rest of her days there, in a room shaded by drawn blinds to ease her old eyes, which were losing their sight. She had a formal reconciliation with Robert. Her spirit was calm and content, and she found a great favorite in a youth who was her sister's grandson, keeping up a charming correspondence with him until the time of her death. On Sunday evening, July 16, 1882, she died, a distinctly old and weary woman, though in only her sixty-fourth year, and was buried beside Lincoln in Oak Ridge Cemetery, Springfield.

Photo by Winfred "Doc" Helm and Arthur "Boots" Holland

Grateful citizens from far and near contributed to the building fund for the magnificent tomb which rises majestically over Lincoln's grave in Oak Ridge Cemetery at Springfield, Illinois. Here also are buried Mrs. Lincoln and their sons Eddie, Willie, and Tad. Robert Lincoln is interred at Arlington National Cemetery, having served as a Captain during the Civil War with General U.S. Grant. A million people each year visit the Lincoln Tomb, which is now owned by the State of Illinois.

SALIENT FACTS ABOUT PRESIDENT LINCOLN AND HIS FAMILY

ABRAHAM LINCOLN (Republican) 1861-(April 15)
1865
Born February 12, 1809, in Hardin Co., Ky.
Son of Thomas and Nancy Hanks Lincoln
Married Mary Todd, 11/4/1842; 4 children
Lawyer
Commissioned as captain in Illinois Militia, 4/7/1832
Volunteered for Black Hawk War, 1832
Unsuccessful candidate Illinois House of Representatives, 1832
Member Illinois General Assembly, 1834-42
Member U.S. House of Representatives, 1847-49
Defeated by Stephen A. Douglas, 1858, for U.S. Senate
Died April 15, 1865, the morning after he was shot by the assassin
    John Wilkes Booth
Landmarks:
The reputed cabin where Lincoln was born, near Hodgenville, Ky.
The Lincoln Home, Springfield, Ill. (8th and Jackson Sts.)
Lincoln Tomb, Oak Ridge Cemetery, Springfield
Lincoln's New Salem. State Park, near Petersburg, Ill., has the rebuilt village
    of New Salem, where Lincoln lived as a young man
William Peterson House, where Lincoln died, Washington, D.C.,
    opposite Lincoln Museum (Ford's Theatre)
Vice President, First Term
Hannibal Hamlin
Vice President, Second Term
Andrew Johnson
Cabinet
Secy of State: William Henry Seward, 3/5/1861
Secy of the Treasury: Salmon Portland Chase, 3/5/1861; William
    Pitt Fessenden, 7/1/1864; Hugh McCulloch, 3/7/1865
Secy of War: Simon Cameron, 3/5/1861; Edwin McMasters Stanton,
    1/15/1862
Atty Gen.: Edward Bates, 3/5/1861; James Speed, 12/2/1864
Postmaster Gen.: Montgomery Blair, 3/5/1861; William Dennison,
    7/24/1864
Secy of the Navy: Gideon Welles, 3/5/1861
Secy of the Interior: Caleb Blood Smith, 3/5/1861; John Palmer
    Usher, 1/1/1863

1860 Election	Electoral Vote	Popular Vote
Abraham Lincoln (Republican)	180	1,866,352
John C. Breckinridge (Southern Democrat)	72	845,763
Stephen A. Douglas (Northern Democrat)	12	1,375,157
John Bell (Constitutional Union Party)	39	589,581

State vote: Lincoln carried Oregon, California, Minnesota, Iowa, Wisconsin,
Illinois, Michigan, Indiana, Ohio, New York, Pennsylvania, Vermont, New Hamp-

54

shire, Maine, Massachusetts, Rhode Island, Connecticut and part of New Jersey.
Breckinridge carried Texas, Arkansas, Louisiana, Mississippi, Alabama, Georgia, South Carolina, North Carolina and Florida, Maryland and Delaware.
Bell and Everett (the Constitutional Union ticket) won Virginia, Kentucky and Tennessee. Douglas carried Missouri and part of the electoral vote of New Jersey.

1864 (Eleven Confederate States not voting)	Electoral Vote	Popular Vote
Abraham Lincoln (Republican)	212	2,216,067
George B. McClellan (Democrat)	21	1,808,725

MARY ANN TODD LINCOLN, generally called Molly
Born December 13, 1818, in Lexington, Ky.
Daughter of Robert Smith and Eliza Ann Parker Todd
Lost her mother when she was 7; father remarried 16 months later
Attended Dr. John Ward's Academy and Madame Mentelle's
    finishing school
Moved to her sister Lizzie's Springfield home in 1839
Married Abraham Lincoln 11/4/1842
First child, Robert Todd, born 8/1/1843, died 7/26/1926
Moved to their Jackson Street home, purchased in 1844
Second child, Edward Baker, born 3/10/1846, died 2/1/1850
Spent winter of 1847 in Washington with the boys, during
    Lincoln's term as a member of the House of Representatives
Third son, William Wallace, born 12/21/1850, died 2/20/1862,
    at the White House
Fourth son, Thomas Wallace, nicknamed Tad, born 4/4/1853,
    died 7/15/1871
First Lady 3/4/1861—4/15/65
Moved to Chicago 5 weeks after Lincoln's death
Agreed to a public sale of her White House finery, 1867,
    then withdrew, bitterly humiliated by publicity created
Left America with Tad 10/1/1868, and stayed in Europe nearly
    three years
Adjudged insane 5/19/1875 and committed to a sanitarium
Allowed to live in the custody of her sister Elizabeth Edwards at
    Springfield in September 1875
Adjudged sane, 6/15/1876
Moved to Europe and remained until October 1880
Died at her sister's home in Springfield, 7/16/1882.

ROBERT TODD LINCOLN
The only child of Abraham and Mary Lincoln who reached maturity
Born 8/1/1843, in Springfield, Ill.
Attended Illinois State University, 1853-59
Failed entrance exams for Harvard, 1859
Entered Exeter Academy instead, where his father visited him on the
    occasion of his Cooper Union address
Attended Harvard, 1861-64
Entered Harvard Law School, 9/5/1864
Appointed captain and assistant adjutant-general of Volunteers by
    General Grant, 2/11/65
Admitted to Illinois bar, 2/25/1867
Married Mary Eunice Harlan, 9/24/1868; 3 children
Elected Supervisor of the town of South Chicago, April 1876
Served as one of the electors on the Republican ticket for the State
    of Illinois, thus participating in the election of Garfield and
    Arthur.

Appointed Secretary of War by President Garfield, 3/5/1881, in which
office he served for 4 years
Witnessed Garfield's assassination, 7/2/1881
Appointed Minister to the Court of St. James by President Harrison;
served 1889-93
Entered into business on his return in preference to the law.
Awarded Degree of Doctor of Laws from Harvard, 1893
Appointed President of the Pullman Company, 1897-1911
Witnessed President McKinley's assassination, 9/6/1901
Died of cerebral hemorrhage, 7/26/1926

CIVIL WAR BATTLES*

Among the most important battles after that of Bull Run in Virginia, 7/21/1861,
were those fought, in 1862, at Fort Donelson, Tenn., 2/14-16; off Hampton Roads,
Va., between the ironclad vessels *Monitor* (Union) and *Merrimac* (Confederate), 3/9;
at Shiloh, Pa., 4/6-7; the capture of New Orleans, 4/29; the second battle of Bull
Run, 8/30; at Antietam, Md., 9/17; Fredericksburg, Va., 12/13; and Mur-
freesborough, Tenn., 12/31-1/2/1863. In 1863, those at Chancellorsville, Va., 5/1-4;
the siege of Vicksburg, Miss., 5/18-7/4; the battle of Gettysburg, Pa., 7/1-3; at
Chickamauga, Ga., 9/19-20; and at Chattanooga, Tenn., 11/23-25. In 1864, in
Virginia, the battles of the Wilderness 5/5-6; at Spottsylvania, 5/8-21; at Cold
Harbor, 6/3; the naval battle of Mobile Bay, 8/5; Sheridan's Shenandoah Valley
campaign in October, Sherman's capture of Atlanta and march through Georgia,
ending in the capture of Savannah, 12/20; and finally, in 1865, the surrender of
Richmond and Petersburg (besieged since the previous June), 4/2-3; and Lee's
formal surrender at Appomattox, 4/7, followed by Johnston's surrender to Sherman
shortly after Lincoln was assassinated.

*Information obtained from: Rhodes, *History of the Civil War* (see bibl.).

NOTES ON THE ILLUSTRATIONS

The first name that comes to mind with regard to photography during the Civil War,
is that of Mathew Brady. Born in Cork, Ireland, about 1823, he was the first to
conceive the idea of taking pictures of actual battles in progress.

He became a protege of Samuel B. Morse and through him met the inventor of
the daguerreotype. From then on Brady was wholly devoted to photography. By
1851 he had studios in New York and in Washington, D.C., and several excellent
men working under him. Wet-plate negatives came into use around 1853. With these,
instead of a single likeness, several copies could be made of each negative. In his
studios Brady often used a multiple lens camera that would take four images on one
plate that was moved quickly while the sitter was still posing.

The stereoscopic camera was a further development. It was used for many Civil
War pictures by Brady and his co-workers. The photograph Alexander Gardner
took of Lincoln with General McClellan (see page 15) is one of these. The camera
took a double image about 2½ inches apart and gave a three-dimensional effect
when looked at through a stereopticon.

Brady initiated battle photography at Bull Run. His standard equipment
became a horse-drawn wagon outfitted with necessary chemicals and glass plates for
the wet-photo process and a curtained compartment for developing pictures. It also
carried an auxiliary tent, which was portable but large enough to house the
cumbersome camera and developing equipment. Plates had to be sensitized just
before exposure, the lens was uncapped by hand, and the negative developed within
five minutes of exposure. Just as war correspondents today are often in danger
themselves, Brady ran great risks. One can imagine, also, that breakage of the glass
negatives must have been frequent, for the wagons went everywhere. Nevertheless an
amazing number of fine photographs (generally after-battle scenes, or pictures of

men in camp) remain as proof of Brady's and his team's courage and persistence.
Brady's attempt to cover the whole war cost him his business. He was forced into bankruptcy in 1872, and although the Library of Congress finally bought most of his plates, the purchase came too late. His Washington gallery was closed in 1881, and until he died in 1896, a forgotten man in a charity hospital, Brady spent his time working for other firms and brooding over his misfortunes.

Many more than the eleven photographs of Lincoln credited to Brady himself were taken at his studios, including all those attributed to Anthony Berger, who was one of his assistants, and many of those by Alexander Gardner, who photographed Lincoln both under Brady's direction and after he had a studio of his own.

Alexander Hesler was Lincoln's campaign photographer (see frontispiece). He was asked to take some poses that would show Lincoln more favorably than in his usual tousled-hair aspect, and he took five pictures in all.

A number of the cartoons we have used are taken from Albert Shaw's *Abraham Lincoln, A Cartoon History,* now in public domain. In relation to the one on page 11 entitled "The Rail Splitter" Shaw writes: "Richard J. Oglesby, a friend of Lincoln's who afterward became Governor, happened to discover that Lincoln in his youth had been employed to split rails on a farm in the Decatur vicinity. He found John Hanks, Lincoln's kinsman and fellow-worker of those early days, and together they brought two or three rails into the convention, carrying a banner upon which was inscribed: 'ABRAHAM LINCOLN the Rail Candidate for President in 1860.' The convention was in the mood for something of this kind, and its endorsement of Lincoln was wildly enthusiastic. . . . At the opening of the campaign the cartoonists caught and made convenient use of this emblem."

Shaw knew the German-born Baltimore dentist Adalbert J. Volck (see cartoons, pp. 16, 43), purchased his portfolio of Lincoln engravings, and used some of them for the first time in his book, as in the case of the one on page 16.

John Tenniel (1820-1914) became more famous later on in the United States as the illustrator for *Alice in Wonderland.* But from May 11, 1861, through February 1865, his cartoons lampooned Lincoln unmercifully in the British journal *Punch.* Shaw used many of them to illustrate his history. (See pp. 14, 19.)

SELECTED BIBLIOGRAPHY
Mr. Lincoln
Angle, Paul M. and Earl S. Miers, eds., *The Living Lincoln: The Man, His Mind, His Times, and the War He Fought, Reconstructed from His Own Writings.* New Brunswick, N. J.: Rutgers University Press, 1955.
Bishop, James A., *The Day Lincoln Was Shot.* New York: Harper and Brothers, 1955.
Duff, John J., *A.Lincoln: Prairie Lawyer.* New York: Rinehart, 1960.
Hamilton, Charles and Lloyd Ostendorf, *Lincoln in Photographs.* Norman: University of Oklahoma Press, 1963
Lorant, Stefan, *Lincoln. A Picture Story of His Life.* New York: W. W. Norton Inc., 1969.
Luthin, Reinhard H., *The Real Abraham Lincoln.* New York: Prentice-Hall, 1960.
Miller, Francis T., Robert S. Lanier *et al,* eds., *The Photographic History of the Civil War.* (New York: Patriot Publishing Co., 1911-12. 10 vols.
Nicolay, John G. and John Hay, *Abraham Lincoln.* 1890. 10 vols. Also *A Short Life of Abraham Lincoln.* New York: Century Co., 1902. 1 vol.
Randall, James G., *Lincoln the President* (4v., 4th vol. with Richard N. Current.) New York: Dodd, Mead & Co., 1945-55
Rhodes, James Ford, *History of the Civil War, 1861-1865.* New York: The MacMillan Company, 1917.
Roscoe, Theodore, *The Web of Conspiracy: The Complete Story of the Men Who Murdered Abraham Lincoln.* Englewood Cliffs, N.J.: Prentice-Hall, 1959.
Sandburg, Carl, *Abraham Lincoln, The Prairie Years.* New York: Harcourt, Brace & Co., 1926

Stephenson, Nathaniel W., *Lincoln*. Indianapolis: The Bobs - Merrill Co., 1922

Tarbell, Ida. *The Life of Abraham Lincoln*. New York: The MacMillan Co., 1917. 2 vols.

Thomas, Benjamin P., *Abraham Lincoln, a Biography*. New York: Alfred A. Knopf, 1952.

The President's Wife and Family:

Colman, Edna. *Seventy-five Years of White House Gossip, from Washington to Lincoln*. Garden City, N. Y.: Doubleday, Page & Co., 1925.

Crook, William H. *Memories of the White House: the Home Life of our Presidents from Lincoln to Roosevelt*. Ed. Henry Rood. Boston: Little, Brown & Co., 1911.

Furman, Bess, *White House Profile: A Social History of the White House*. Indianapolis, Ind.: The Bobs-Merrill Co., 1951.

Jensen, Amy La Follette, *The White House and Its Thirty-Three Families*. New York: McGraw-Hill Book Co., 1962.

Langford, Laura C. H. *The Ladies of the White House*. New York: United States Pub. Co., 1870.

McConnell, Jane, and Burt McConnell, *Our First Ladies, from Martha Washington to Mamie Eisenhower*. New York: Thomas Y. Crowell Co., 1957.

Perling, Joseph, *Presidents' Sons*. New York: Odyssey Press, 1947.

Poore, Ben. Perley, Perley's *Reminiscences of Sixty Years in the National Metropolis*. Philadelphia, Hubbard Bros., 1886.

Prindiville, Kathleen, *First Ladies*. New York: The MacMillan Co., 1954.

Randall, Ruth Painter, *Lincoln's Sons*. New York: The MacMillan Co., 1917.

Randolph, Mary, *Presidents and First Ladies*. New York: D. Appleton-Century Co., 1936.

Sweetser, Kate D. *Famous Girls of the White House*. New York: Thomas Y. Crowell Co., 1937.

Truett, Randle B. *The First Ladies in Fashion*. With fashion notes by Philip Robertson. New York: Hastings House, 1954. (On the Smithsonian collection of First Ladies' dresses.)

Washington Merry-Go-Round. New York: Horace Liveright, 1931

White, William Allen, *Masks in a Pageant*. New York. The Macmillan Co., 1929

White House Historical Association. *The White House, an Historic Guide*. Washington: 1962

Mary Lincoln:

Angle, Paul M. *"Here I have lived"; a history of Lincoln's Springfield, 1821-1865*. Springfield, Ill.: The Abraham Lincoln Association, 1935.

Evans, William A. *Mrs. Abraham Lincoln, a Study of Her Personality and Her Influence on Lincoln*. New York: Alfred A. Knopf, 1932.

Helm, Katherine. *The True Story of Mary, Wife of Lincoln: containing the recollections of Mary Lincoln's sister Emilie (Mrs. Ben Hardin Helm), extracts from her wartime diary, numerous letters and other documents now first publ. by her niece*. New York: Harper & Bros. 1928.

Keckley, Elizabeth Hobbs. *Behind the Scenes; or Thirty years a slave, and four years in the White House*. New York: G. W. Carleton, 1868. By Mrs. Lincoln's dressmaker-companion.

Morrow, Honoré McCue W. *Mary Todd Lincoln; an Appreciation of the Wife of Abraham Lincoln*. New York: W. Morrow, 1928.

Randall, Ruth Painter. *Mary Lincoln; Biography of a Marriage*. Boston: Little, Brown & Co., 1953.

Sandburg, Carl, and Angle, Paul M. *Mary Lincoln, Wife and Widow*. Part I by Sandburg; Part II, letters, documents and appendix, by Angle. New York: Harcourt, Brace & Co., 1932

Tarbell, Ida M. *In the Footsteps of the Lincolns*. New York: Harper and Bros., 1924

The quotations from Lincoln's autobiography (bottom pp. 8, 9); his editorial offered to the editors of the *Illinois Journal* (bottom pp. 10, 11); his first inaugural address (bottom p. 13); the Emancipation Proclamation (bottom p. 19); his second inaugural (bottom pp. 22, 23); and his Gettysburg address were taken from *The Living Lincoln* (see bibl.).